Praise for THE FACES OF GUAN YIN

"Dennis Maloney's poem-glimpses of the fascinating Buddhist figure of Guan Yin draw richly on an almost infinite set of teaching stories and folk tales. Maloney's poems offer a many-sided, personal, and idiosyncratic introduction to this shape-shifting, gender-shifting embodiment of freed thought, feeling, and action. These poems hold a much-needed, supple, inventive reminder of the central teaching of all Buddhism, as held by Guan Yin: that the key to ending suffering is an untethered, unstinting, unlimiting, and utterly unconventional compassion."

~ Jane Hirshfield

"Exquisite and powerful poems about and inspired by the great compassionate Guan Yin, these poems by Dennis Maloney open the door of compassion."

~ Roshi Joan Halifax, Abbot,
Upaya Zen Center

The Faces of Guan Yin

Dennis Maloney

with art by

Mayumi Oda

Folded Word
Meredith, New Hampshire

Number 57 of 100

ISBN: 978-1-61019-245-3

Folded Word
79 Tracy Way
Meredith, NH 03253
United States of America
WWW.FOLDEDWORD.COM

"Hands of Compassion" (cover art) and black & white drawings by Mayumi Oda, used with her generous permission. FMI: mayumioda.net

Author portrait by Elaine LaMattina

98765432 FIRST PRINTING

To the often hidden female lineage of Buddhism,
to the many goddesses in everyday life,
and to the feminine in all of us.

Contents

List of Artwork	viii
Preface	ix
Acknowledgements	xii
The Faces of Guan Yin	1
Notes	47
About the Author	49
About the Press	51
Colophon	54

List of Artwork

Hands of Compassion	cover
untitled	xi
untitled	2
She Carries Me	45

Preface

Guan Yin is the embodiment of compassion and wisdom in Buddhism and is said to be the protector of women, children, sailors, fishermen, the sick, those in trouble, and the poor. She is the one who "hears the cries of the world." She is considered a bodhisattva, one who foregoes enlightenment until all sentient beings are liberated. She is said to manifest in a variety of forms to free beings from suffering. Originally depicted in India as a male or androgynous figure, by the time Buddhism reached China and elsewhere Guan Yin had evolved to a female form.

These poems explore Guan Yin in the historic context of various female roles and figures in Buddhism, as well as in responses to contemporary events and situations. Some poems are in her voice or in the voice of historic female figures in Buddhism, and others are petitions to her.

Known by many names
manifested as:

Avalokiteshvara in India
Kannon in Japan
Guan Yin in China
Chenrezig in Tibet
Quan Am in Vietnam
Gwan Eum in Korea
Kuan Im in Thailand
that spoke the heart sutra

androgynous or
female appearing in
a myriad of forms
through the ages
not a god
but guide

please guide us
through samsara

Mayumi

Acknowledgements

With thanks to many teachers: Robert Aitken Roshi, the Kahawai Collective (A Buddhist women's collective at the Diamond Sangha who were among the first to identify the lineage of women teachers in Buddhism), Jikan-sensei, and Mayumi Oda. And to the following authors whose books inspired some of these poems: Sarah E. Truman, Sandy Boucher, John Blofeld, Grace Schireson, and Taigen Dan Leighton.

With gratitude to John Brandi, Renee Gregorio, and especially Elaine LaMattina for looking at early versions of these poems and for their suggestions on the poems and their ordering.

~Dennis Maloney
January 2019

No book is possible without the people of its press. The author and publisher would like to thank Rose Auslander, whose editorial efforts expedited the publication of this book, as well as Zakariah Johnson, Casey Tingle, Sarah Gibson, Barbara Flaherty, Kristine Slentz, Caroline Fout, Tobi Carter, Heidi Marshall, and Claire Graustein for their assistance at the press during its production.

Versions of some of the poems have appeared in the following magazines and anthologies:

Pirene's Fountain, the *Esalen* catalog, *Southern Florida Review*, *Water* (A Poet Speaks Anthology), *Trumped* (A Poet Speaks Anthology), and the *Sexuality Poems Anthology*.

The Faces of Guan Yin

Mayumi

1

In stories we may see you
as an old woman serving tea
at a roadside stand to travelers
who enter with a thirst.

Fragrant green tea appears.
Those who enter filled
with arrogance and ego
are chased away.

Su Tung Po read his poems
to the tea lady and if she
didn't understand them,
he would rewrite them.

She serves tea and wipes
the counter with a clean rag,
the unrecognized teacher
outside the gate.

Miaozong inquires of the head monk:

Does the Buddhadharma distinguish
between male and female form?

Will this be a dharma
interview or a worldly interview?

The head monk replies, “A dharma interview.”

Then ask your attendants to leave
and please come in.

When he opened the curtain, Miaozong
was lying face up, naked, on the bed.

“What kind of place is this?” he asks.

Miaozong responds:

The buddhas of the three worlds,
the six patriarchs and all great monks
come from within.

He asks, "Will you allow me to enter?"

Horses may cross but not asses.

This interview is over.

3

In 628 A.D.
two fisherman netted
a small golden Kannon
while fishing
and built a small hut
to enshrine it in what
is now Senso-ji,
one of the oldest
temples in Tokyo.

She has remained
hidden since,
deep in the Buddha hall.

Through clouds of incense,
crowds ascend and ascend the stone steps,
drop a few coins in the bin,
bow and clap their hands.

4

You sit in zazen
on a seat of lotus leaves
in a grotto of rough rock,
tree roots snaking
though the stones.

Night rain washes
down the mountain,
at dawn everything
green soaked through.

Swirling curves
of energy
strata of bedrock,
a cool breeze,
flowing water,
tongues of flame.

Place of spirits,
passage between worlds,
roaming free, a full moon
deep in the mountains.

5

The tea cake lady asks Deshan

What are you carrying?

Deshan replies "Commentaries
on the diamond sutra."

She says, *I have a question for you.*
If you answer it I will give you a pastry.
If not you'll have to buy it elsewhere.

The diamond sutra says
past mind can't be grasped,
present mind can't be grasped,
future mind can't be grasped,
What mind does the learned
monk wish to enlighten?

6

A vision of Kyoto
as seen at Sanjusangen-do Temple:
Senju Kannon,
thousand armed,

hands holding
bells, wands, flowers, a factory,
waterfalls, mountains,
vajra thunderbolts, lovers, flags,

daggers, the Sanjo Street bridge,
streetcars, tiny stone gardens,
coffeehouses, bars, shops,
a grid of streets, prayer beads,

monks intoning sutras
before dawn,
ashes of friends,
samurai ghosts roaming the streets,

the textile looms of Nishijin,
Toyota taxis, vases, ancient temples,
high rise apartments,
conch shell trumpets, the bullet train,

a fistful of snow, rice paddies,
books, bottles, Dharma wheels,
the wash under the eaves.

.

7

White robe Guan Yin
One leaf Guan Yin
Moon-water Guan Yin
Horse head Guan Yin

Rock cave Guan Yin
Wish-fulfilling gem Guan Yin
Fish basket Guan Yin
Calming Guan Yin

Leaf robed Guan Yin
Pure water Guan Yin
Lotus holding Guan Yin
Extending life Guan Yin

Blue-necked Guan Yin
Nonduality Guan Yin
Fearless Guan Yin
Clam Guan Yin
Child providing Guan Yin

Guan Yin holding a sutra
Guan Yin holding a willow branch
Guan Yin of complete light
Guan Yin viewing waterfalls
One Guan Yin

8

Why does Guan Yin have
so many hands and eyes?

It's like reaching back for
your pillow in the dark.

Do you understand?

The whole body is covered
with hands and eyes.

Almost.

Then what do you say?

There's nothing but hands and eyes.

9

Young and intoxicated
with my own lovely skin,
figure and flawless face,
dressed to kill, despised
by other woman, I
hunted fools
in the marketplace of love.

Head shaved,
wearing robes,
wandering for alms,
I am myself,
no thought,
unbound, without
men or possessions,
those fires
quenched.

10

I used to be
fragrant as
scented oak with
flowers in my hair.
With old age
I smell like a damp,
matted dog.

My body once
a palace of pleasure
now a house
of pain,
plaster sloughing off.

11

Raging flame consumes
fifty homes in a flash,
creeps up and down
mountainsides.

Rooted in solid ground
your wings spread, rising
through the inferno,
heat waves undulating in the air
as if space could shift.

Weeks later,
here we stand taking
the bitter taste into our lungs
eyes straining to find the
familiar, charred black trunks
against stark white ash.

If our lives burn well, will we
find poetry in the ashes?

12

I first heard your mantra
chanting as Allen Ginsberg
pumped his harmonium
on the floor of the Everson
Art Museum, Syracuse, 1971,

calming the crowd there
to see John Lennon & Yoko Ono
and rumors of a Beatles reunion
for John's 31st birthday.

The crowd becoming
one body, one trembling sound

behold the jewel in the lotus

om mani padme hum

om mani padme hum

my innermost door
opening just a crack
the first time.

13

In a book of goddesses
the poet found a photo
of the Tibetan goddess Tara,
the most beautiful woman
he had ever seen, he thought.

She who is the mother
of the buddhas,
of wisdom and compassion,
with a body of dew,
a face peaceful and smiling,
a tremendous white light
dissolving illusions.

Every once in a while
he would open the book
and look at Tara, and wonder
where she was these days,
how she was getting on.

14

You may only glimpse
her once or twice
in your life, maybe
at a concert, maybe
the Grateful Dead
or Carlos Santana,

swaying to the band,
seduced by the
guitar singing,
moving inside riffs,
punctuating the beat,
her body sliding
between notes,

unfiltered,
surrendering to
gravity and music,
she is flying,

the walls dancing,
the music giving way.
Transcendence.

15

To reassert their power,
the old men
embrace the twins
of ignorance and arrogance,
find the key to reopen
the half-buried trunks
of hate and bigotry,

summoning darkness
they use our language to manipulate,
distort, deny, and betray.
The judge
renders his verdict:
there was no
terrorist among us.

Do you hear us knocking?

16

Two monks traveling
together come to a
river with a strong
current. As they
prepare to cross they
see a young beautiful
woman who asks
their help to cross.

Even though they have
taken a vow not to
touch a woman, one
monk picks her up and
carries her across the river.

Hours later down the trail
one monk says to the other:
As monks we are not
permitted to touch a woman.
How could you carry her?

The other replies:
I set her down on
the other side
of the river. Why
are you still carrying her?

17

Cherry blossoms hang
from mountain pillows,
my heart threadbare
as they fall
this evening.

In the autumn of life
Rengetsu wrote to another,
said she was under the weather,
often just lying in her hut

she thought it would be
good to die but
then the wind cools,
she hears the cries of wild geese,
watches the moon alone.

18

In Noh plays there is
always a traveler,
usually a monk,
who encounters
an ethereal woman

often appearing in
a dream as a ghost
or spirit of a poet,
plum tree, dancer in
a feathery robe,

a mad woman
scooping cherry blossoms
from the stream
who later transforms
into an old woman
mountain spirit
serving dinner
at a mountain inn.

19

Pondering this and that
you try to keep the
bucket together
but the bottom
keeps falling out.

Where water
doesn't collect,
the moon
won't dwell.

When the bottom
fell out, the pale
moon of dawn
was caught
in the rain puddle
that never
seems to fade.

20

She weaves
words to fill the books
of question and failure,

the way the spider
spends all night
spinning a web that turns
into a jeweled net
glistening with beads
of dew at dawn.

21

Some days our world
seems to unravel,
a coup here, a flood there,
earthquakes, tornadoes,
suicide bombers blossom
violently in Paris, Istanbul,
Bali, Kabul, Baghdad.

We seem to careen from
catastrophe to catastrophe—
a voice at sea crying
in the night, a gunman
walking into a classroom.

How can you contain
these multitudes?

22

In the wind
your voice
reverberates crystal in each
secret heart chamber,
the whole body
becoming an ear.

All creatures
fall silent
inside the cave
of their hearts,
inside their hearing,
a temple.

The clarity
of a star-filled night,
snowfall blanketing
the earth.

23

Songs of incantation,
songs of despair, some days
we swallow the bitter
taste of this rusted-out life
until we can swallow no more—

burnt, broken,
torn at the seams,
we carry a dark shadow
in the softness of our body,
yet the world goes on.

I look not to see
the damage but
the mended breaks,
the repairs that have
made you more beautiful.

24

Goddess, you belong to the night.
Do you hear our prayers
or our melancholy praise?

Allow us
to slip beneath
the meaning in our dreams,
the secrets our bodies hold.
Encourage our dance.

Last night I heard your voice,
your words singing to me.
Let us all have that moment
when we choose to surrender.

25

She places her hands
gently on your shoulders,
pulls you close,
whispers in your ear:

Say goodbye.
to the pain that forms
around the heart,
to fears and insecurities,
to chaos, glamour,
to the vehicle that carried
you on so many journeys.

Forget you are a beautiful disaster,
a train careening out
of control.
Slip out of the armor
you think protects you.

To be human is to
embark on that most
profound pilgrimage
to the temple within.

26

When we confine you
to the altar we miss
the chance to see you
in your various guises.

Through the music
of the ordinary sounds
of this world, we find you.

The ancient hotel heater
in Amsterdam playing
what sounds like an
Indian raga.

A mother singing
an old folksong
to soothe her daughter
to sleep on the
cross-country flight.

The cacophony of the
Shanghai train station
speakers blaring
incomprehensible commands
over the din of the crowd.

In the fields, the mountains,
the flowers, in my body, too,
sound flows constantly like
a stream in a mountain valley
or the stream of city traffic.

Between bell and fish drum
I almost catch
a whiff of your fragrance.

27

Goddess of rivers and oceans
with all those arms,
are you strong enough
to hold the earth together
in its slow collapse?

Bathed in warm water
the vibrant colors fade
from the Great Barrier Reef,
bleached coral dying.

From the streams of the Dakotas
to the homes in Flint,
to the plateaus of Tibet,
rivers stink, full of
dead fish and yaks.

From the Bering Strait
to the islands of the South Pacific,
the ocean eats at the edges
of the land.

A luxury cruise ship finds
a path through the Northwest Passage.
In Miami, they are raising
the streets to cope
with the rising tide.

When the Japanese
mended a prized ceramic, they
filled the cracks with gold
to call attention to the
brokenness of the object.

Is there gold to fill
the cracks we have made
in the beauty of this world?

一葉観音
She carries me

Notes

"Known by many names" — After poet Lew Welch

Samsara refers to the wheel of existence and the cycles of birth and death.

Miaozong (1095 – 1170), also known as Wuzhuo, was a Chinese Buddhist nun.

Buddhadharma refers to the teachings of the Buddha and the inner realization of those teachings.

Dharma is the teachings of the Buddha.

Deshan (819 – 914) was a scholar-monk who lectured on the Diamond Sutra in China and was a well-known Zen teacher.

Diamond Sutra is one of the central texts of Mahayana Buddhism. "The diamond that cuts through afflictions, ignorance, illusion, or delusion."

Sanjusangen-do Temple is a temple in Kyoto, Japan, which houses a large statue of the (Senju) thousand-armed Kannon (Guan Yin), and one thousand standing life-size statues of the thousand-armed Kannon.

Rengetsu (1791 – 1875) was a Japanese Buddhist nun who was highly regarded as a poet. She was also a skilled potter and painter and expert calligrapher.

About the Author

Dennis Maloney is a poet and translator. A number of volumes of his own poetry have been published, including *The Map Is Not the Territory: Poems & Translations* and *Just Enough*. His book *Listening to Tao Yuan Ming* was published by Glass Lyre Press in 2015 and a bilingual German/English volume, *Empty Cup*, was published in Germany in 2017. *The Things I Notice Now* was published in 2018 by MadHat Press.

In 2019, a chapbook, *Windows*, with translations in several languages, will appear in Germany from Hochroth Verlag. His works of translation include: *The Stones of Chile* by Pablo Neruda, *The Landscape of Castile* by Antonio Machado, *Between the Floating Mist: Poems of Ryokan*, and *The Poet and the Sea* by Juan Ramon Jimenez.

He is also the editor and publisher of the widely respected White Pine Press in Buffalo, New York, and divides his time between Buffalo, New York, and Big Sur, California.

To learn more, please visit:

WhitePine.org

About the Press

Since 2008, Folded Word has been
exploring the world, one voice at a time
with the help of editors, authors, and readers
who value sustainable literature.

For a complete list of our titles, visit the Folded Word website: *folded.wordpress.com*

To report typographical errors, email:
FoldedEditors@gmail.com

Want more information about our titles? Want to connect with our authors? No problem. Simply join us at a social media outlet near you:

Facebook: *www.facebook.com/foldedword*
Twitter: *twitter.com/foldedword*

FOLDED WORD
is a proud member of

[clmp]

Community of Literary Magazines and Presses
Ensuring a vibrant, diverse literary landscape
WWW.CLMP.ORG

and gives annual support to:

Poets House
A place for poetry: library, literary center, locus of poetic inspiration
WWW.POETSHOUSE.ORG

The Haiku Foundation
Preserving and archiving the first century of haiku in English; providing resources for the next
WWW.THEHAIKUFOUNDATION.ORG

What did you think?

Let us know with a quick rating or review at
www.GoodReads.com
or wherever you search for books.

☆☆☆☆☆

Folded Word reserves a portion of each print run to donate to libraries and reading programs in under-served communities. Please email us at FOLDEDEDITORS@GMAIL.COM *if you would like your organization to be considered.*

Colophon

Cover and textblock design by JS Graustein, featuring the artwork of Mayumi Oda.

The title face is Biographer, designed by Angel Koziupa and Alejandro Paul, issued by Sudtipos in 2010.

The text face is Plantin Pro, designed by Frank Hinman Pierpont, issued by Monotype in 2001.

Supplemental glyphs are Paciencia, designed by Thiago Oliveira, issued by Typographias in 2017.

Printed in the United States of America by Walch Printing of Portland, Maine, on 70# Cougar Natural, an acid-free, FSC® Certified, SFI® Certified Sourcing, and Rainforest Alliance Certified™ sustainable paper.

Endsheets are Construction : Nightshift Blue, a paper produced with recycled fibers via hydropower by French Paper Company in Niles, Michigan.